Copyright ©2021 Charlene A. Ryan

All rights reserved. No part of this book may be reproduced or used in any manner whatsoever without written permission of the copyright owner except for the use of brief quotations in a book review.

First paperback edition September 2021

ISBN (paperback): 978-1-954041-08-0
ISBN (hardback): 978-1-954041-09-7

Published by Creative Sound Press
www.creativesoundpress.com
publishing@creativesoundpress.com

All book and cover art created with
oil on canvas by Charlene A. Ryan.
All rights reserved.

creativesoundpress.com

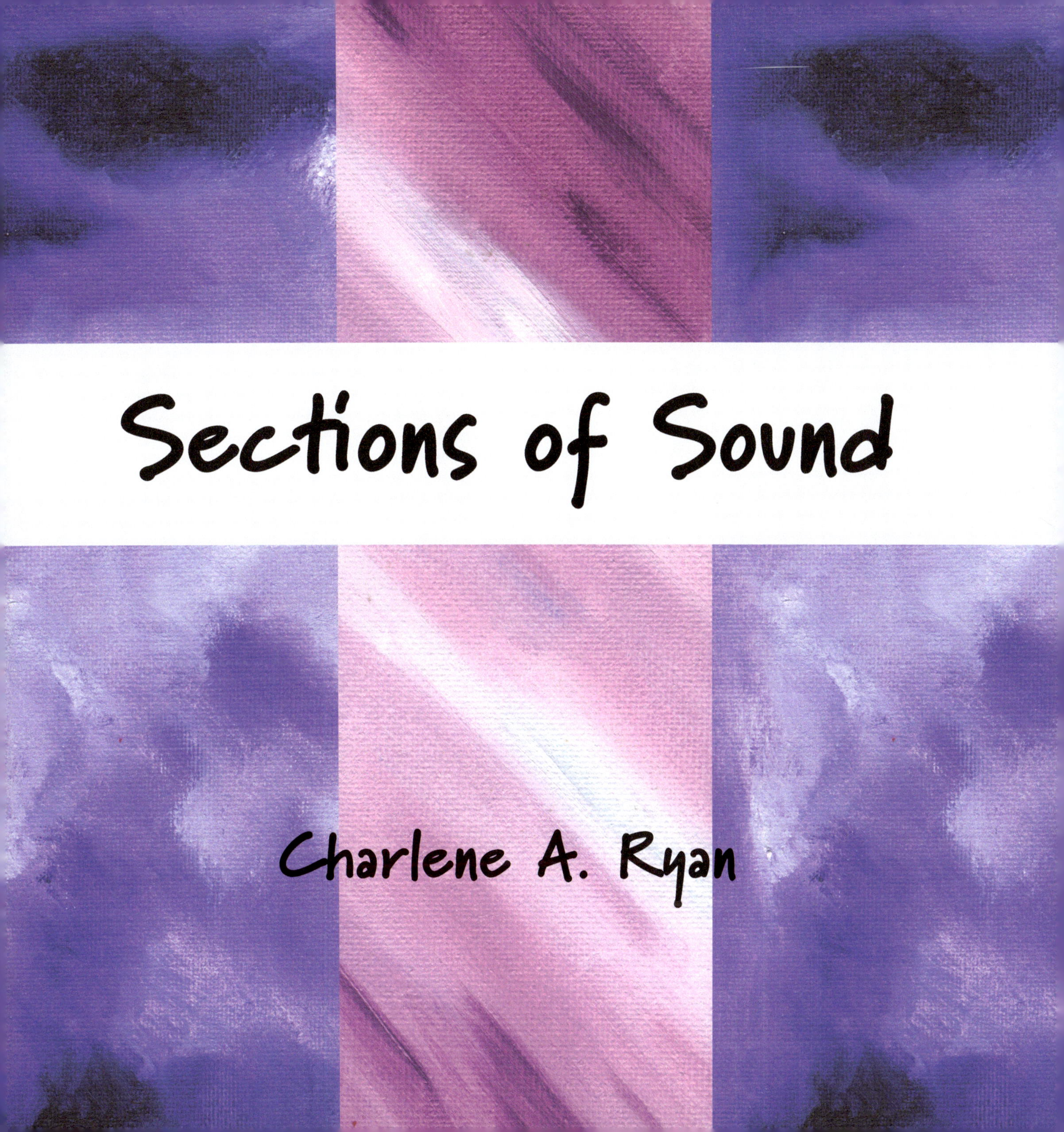

Sections of Sound

Charlene A. Ryan

*For Matthew, Aiden, Audrey Anna, and Amelia Claire.
May every section of your lives be full of beautiful
sounds and colors.*

How to use this book

Each 2-page spread comprises unique combinations of artwork arranged in patterns that represent typical forms of musical structure. They are basic and clear representations of the overall construction of a composition. The images can be used to introduce and illustrate the concept of musical form. They might be employed to guide focus and understanding while listening to musical works that match the forms represented. The artwork also serves as an excellent starting place for the creation of new musical compositions. Encourage children to imagine the sounds they hear in the images and to differentiate the sounds and musical events in each distinct section of artwork. Ask them to consider what vocal sounds they could use, what found sounds work, and what instrument sounds might be effective. And when you've exhausted the book's possibilities, have the children create their own artwork, as a starting point for their musical creativity to unfold!

FORM: AA

FORM: AB

FORM: ABA

FORM: AAA

FORM: ABA

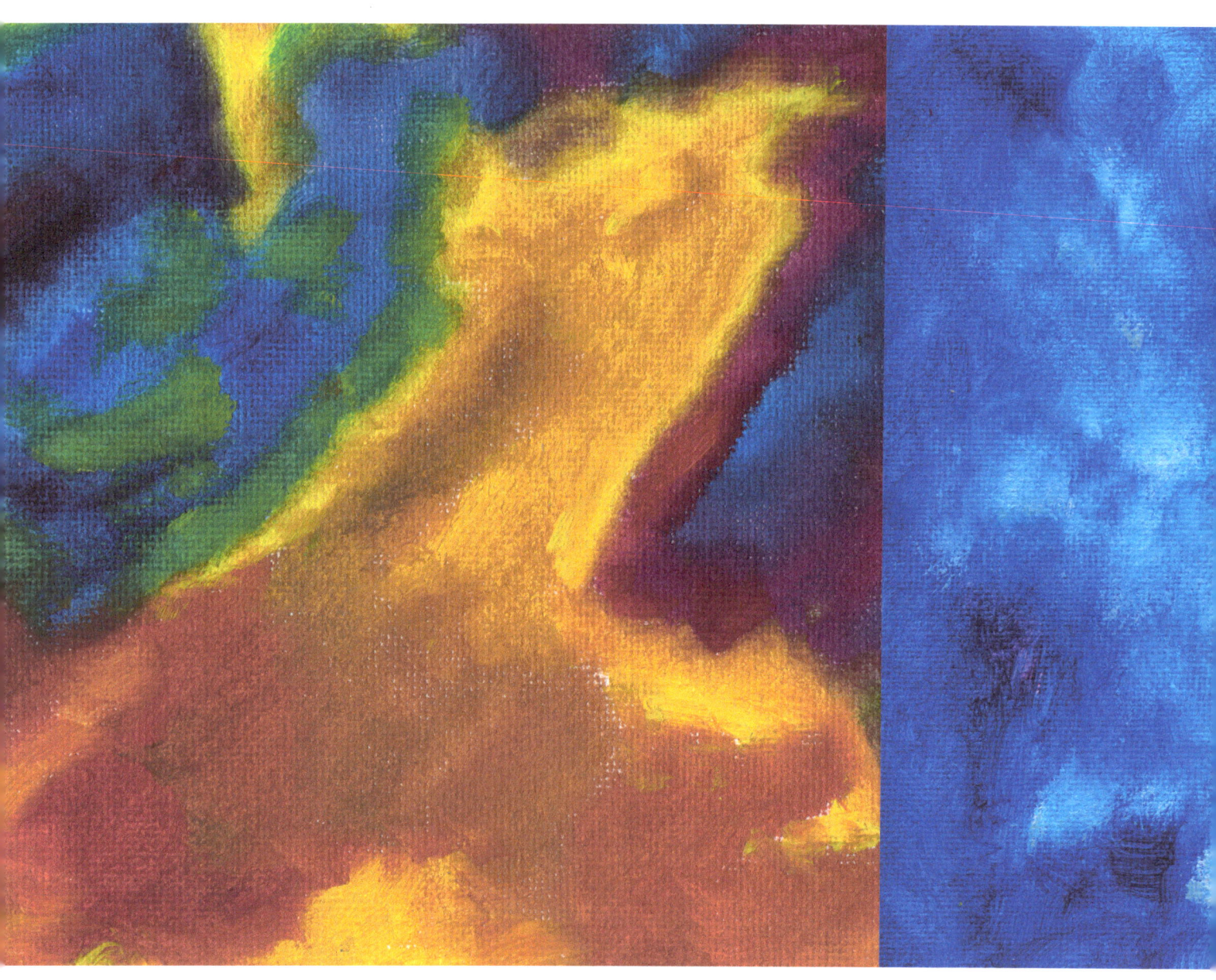

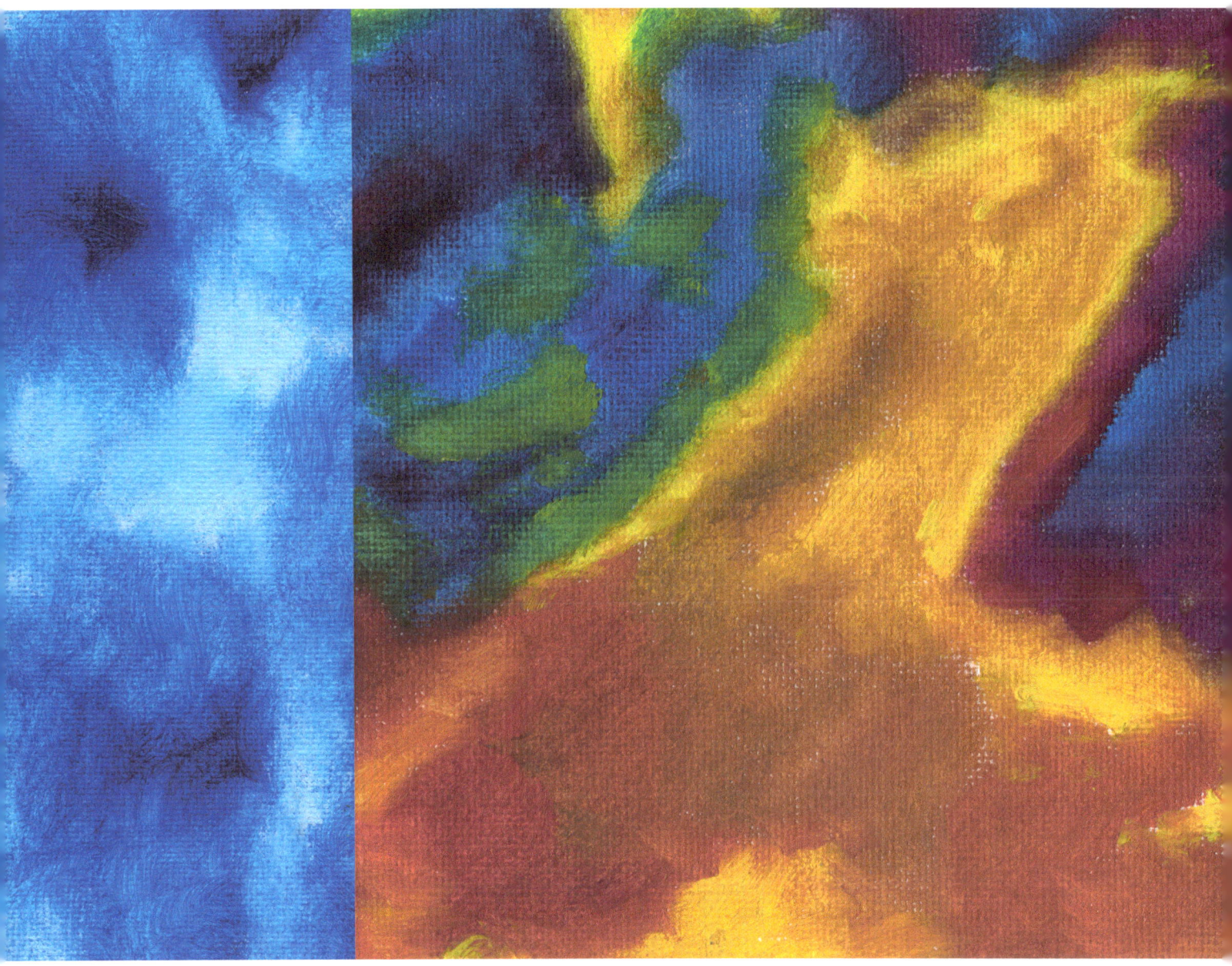

FORM: ABABA

FORM: ABACA

FORM: ABABAB

FORM: ABACABA

FORM: ABABCB

FORM: AABA

FORM: THEME AND VARIATIONS

Charlene A. Ryan is a musician, painter, writer, and mom. She has spent most of her life behind an instrument and in front of an audience of one kind or another.

Other books by Charlene include:
Up and Down Sounds
Big and Small Sounds
Hannabelle's Butterflies
Katherine Lost

To learn more about Charlene and her work, visit www.charlenearyan.com

www.ingramcontent.com/pod-product-compliance
Lightning Source LLC
Chambersburg PA
CBHW041100070526
44579CB00002B/20